A CIP catalogue record for this book is
available from the British Library.
ISBN 07136 3768 4

A&C Black (Publishers) Ltd
35 Bedford Row, London, WC1R 4JH
© 1993 A&C Black (Publishers) Ltd

Acknowledgements

Edited by Barbara Taylor
Mathematics consultant Mike Spooner

The photographer, author and publishers would
like to thank the following people whose help
and co-operation made this book possible:
Louise Kirk, Jake Roberts, Jane Salazar,
Jane Tassie, Taskmaster Ltd, James Galt & Co. Ltd,
the Early Learning Centre.

Typeset by Rowland Phototypesetting Ltd,
Bury St Edmunds, Suffolk.
Printed and bound in Italy by L.E.G.O. Spa

Number puzzles

Rose Griffiths
Photographs by Peter Millard

A & C Black · London

Which numbers are we hiding?

Which number will
I peg up next?

0 2 4

Which number will come up next on my calculator?

Are the numbers getting bigger or smaller?

Which number will I turn over next?

How many bricks do I need
to build the next step?

8

. . . fifteen . . .

Which number will Georgia say next?

I'm making ten snails for a missing number puzzle.

I've hidden some of the snails under this flower pot.

How many snails are hiding?

Were you right?

. . . and she drew one for me.

13

David is making
a puzzle card
with flaps.

Which numbers are
hidden under the flaps?

$$24 + 6 = 30$$

$$\square + 20 = 30$$

$$30 + \square = 30$$

Which numbers could be hidden here?

$$\square + \square = 13$$

Georgia has made a number machine.

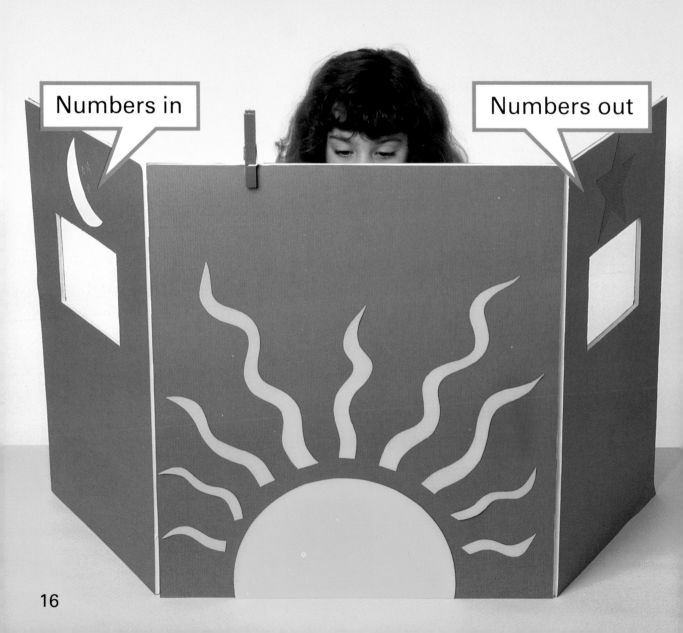

When I put a
number into
her machine . . .

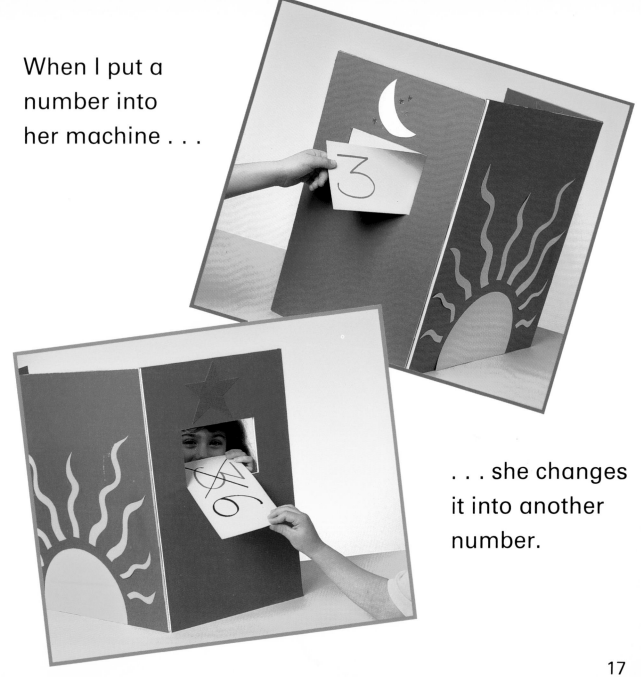

. . . she changes
it into another
number.

What is Georgia doing to the numbers?

19

Now it's David's turn.

He wants to take away
two each time.

. . . which number will he change it into?

We're making up
a car puzzle.

How many cars
shall I hide?

22

Can you make up your own number puzzles?

Try them out on your friends.

More things to do

1. Snakes in the bushes

Draw a snake on a piece of card and write a sequence of numbers along its body. For example, you could write the numbers from the three times table, in order. Cut out a leaf shape from card and use it to cover one of the numbers. Can your friend work out which number is hidden?

2. Calculator sequences

Some types of calculator can make number sequences very easily. You just have to key in a sum, then keep on pressing the equals button and see what appears on the display.

For example, you could key in

| 13 | − | 2 | = | = |

and the display will show 11, then 9, then 7. What do you think will come next? Say what number you think it will be, then press equals to see if you were right. What happens if you keep pressing equals? See if you can make up your own sums and calculator sequences.

Find the page

This list shows you where to find some of the ideas in this book.

Notes for parents and teachers

As you read this book with children, these notes will help you to explain the basic algebra behind the different number puzzles. Algebra uses symbols to represent unknown numbers and explores number patterns and relationships between numbers.

Number sequences Pages 2, 3, 4, 5, 6, 7, 8, 9

A number sequence needs a number to start with and a rule to specify how to continue the sequence. Pages 2 and 3 show the sequence of counting numbers where each number is one more than the last one. The sequences on pages 4 and 5 are made by adding or subtracting two each time. Page 4 shows even numbers and page 5 shows odd numbers. Pages 6 and 7 extend the same theme by adding or subtracting three. On page 7, the first step needs fifteen bricks, the second step twelve and the third step nine. Pages 8 and 9 show multiples of five.

Missing numbers Pages 2, 3, 10, 11, 12, 13, 14, 15, 22, 23

Children are more likely to be successful with missing number problems if they start by using practical equipment instead of numbers and symbols. Use any situation that the child feels happy with, such as snails under a flower pot, cars in a garage, fish hiding behind a rock or teddies hiding under a blanket. Many children will use 'counting on' from the number of objects still visible – perhaps using their fingers – to work out how many are missing. Do not rush a child into subtraction instead.

The 'numbers under flaps' puzzles offer a different way of thinking about combinations of numbers. When one number is hidden by a flap, there is only one possible answer. But when two numbers are hidden, more than one answer could be correct. Until one of the missing numbers has been revealed, the correct answer can only be guessed at.

Children can work on these puzzles with small or large numbers, depending on how confident they are at counting.

Using symbols Pages 13, 14, 15, 22

Encourage children to invent their own symbols to represent missing numbers. The symbols can be based on the shape of the actual objects (such as flower pots) that they are using for their puzzles. The children can use these symbols, along with numbers, pictures and signs such as plus and equals to write down their puzzles.

Number machines Pages 16, 17, 18, 19, 20, 21

A number machine is a way of helping children concentrate on three aspects of a calculation: the input (the number you start with), the function (what you do to the number), and the output (the number you end up with). If you make a number machine, you may find it helpful to use labels for 'in' and 'out'.

The child operating the machine concentrates on calculating the output, as she knows the input and the function. The other children have to guess the function. For example, with an input of three and an output of six, the machine could be multiplying by two or adding three; you need several examples to work out the correct function.

It is also useful to encourage children to work backwards. Tell them the output and the function and see if they can work out the input.